In Praise of
MOTHERS

In Praise of
MOTHERS

NERO

Published by Nero,
an imprint of Schwartz Publishing Pty Ltd
Level 1, 221 Drummond Street
Carlton VIC 3053, Australia
enquiries@blackincbooks.com
www.nerobooks.com

ISBN 9781863959346

Cover design by Peter Long
Text design by Tristan Main
Typeset by Duncan Blachford
Illustrations by UIrtsya, Shutterstock

Printed in China at 1010 International

In Praise of Mothers

Every year in May, we set aside a special day to celebrate
motherhood and mothers, the women who make the world go
round. Humankind has been celebrating mothers for millennia,
through festivals such as the ancient Greek and Roman
celebrations of the fertility goddesses Rhea and Cybele.

Mothers are the making of us, both literally and
emotionally: they shape us, teach us, help us and, most
importantly, they love us and show us how to love others.
The relationship between mother and child is so profound
that we sometimes fail to find the words with which to express
our feelings, and so turn to the words of others. From the
hilarious to the heartfelt, from Sophocles to Sid Vicious,
this collection of quotes celebrates the joy, humour, pain
and wonder of motherhood.

Motherhood: All love begins and ends there.

ROBERT BROWNING

A mother is the truest friend we have,
when trials, heavy and sudden, fall upon us . . .
[she will] dissipate the clouds of darkness,
and cause peace to return to our hearts.

WASHINGTON IRVING

My mother had a great deal of trouble with me,
but I think she enjoyed it.

MARK TWAIN

All that I am, or hope to be,

I owe to my angel mother.

ABRAHAM LINCOLN

We are born of love;

Love is our mother.

RUMI

The natural state of motherhood is unselfishness. When you become a mother, you are no longer the center of your own universe. You relinquish that position to your children.

JESSICA LANGE

What are Raphael's madonnas
but the shadow of a mother's love,
fixed in a permanent outline forever?

T.W. HIGGINSON

The heart of a mother is a deep abyss
at the bottom of which you will always
find forgiveness.

HONORÉ DE BALZAC

A mother's arms are made of tenderness
and children sleep soundly in them.

VICTOR HUGO

Mother's love is peace.
It need not be acquired,
it need not be deserved.

ERICH FROMM

Because I feel that, in the Heavens above
The angels, whispering to one another,
Can find, among their burning terms of love
None so devotional as that of 'Mother' . . .

EDGAR ALLAN POE

[Motherhood is] the biggest gamble in the world.
It is the glorious life force. It's huge and scary —
it's an act of infinite optimism.

GILDA RADNER

When you are a mother, you are never really alone in your thoughts. A mother always has to think twice, once for herself and once for her child.

SOPHIA LOREN

I realized when you look at your mother,
you are looking at the purest love you will ever know.

MITCH ALBOM

Grown don't mean nothing to a mother.
A child is a child. They get bigger, older, but grown.
In my heart it don't mean a thing.

TONI MORRISON

Whatever else is unsure
in this stinking dunghill of a world,
a mother's love is not.

JAMES JOYCE

All women become like their mothers.
That is their tragedy. No man does.
That's his.

OSCAR WILDE

Youth fades; love droops; the leaves of friendship fall;

A mother's secret hope outlives them all.

Oliver Wendell Holmes

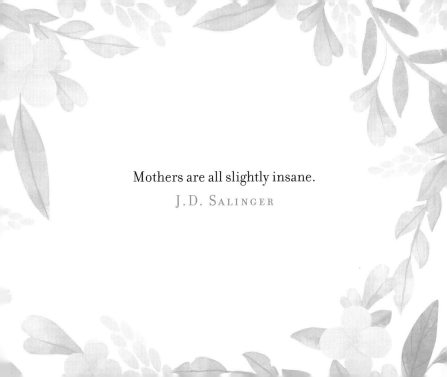

Mothers are all slightly insane.

J.D. SALINGER

A mother's arms are more comforting than anyone else's.

If you bungle raising your children, I don't think
whatever else you do well matters very much.

JACQUELINE KENNEDY ONASSIS

The hand that rocks the cradle
Is the hand that rules the world.

W.R. WALLACE

It may be possible to gild pure gold,
but who can make his mother more beautiful?

MAHATMA GANDHI

Thou art thy mother's glass, and she in thee
Calls back the lovely April of her prime.

WILLIAM SHAKESPEARE

Mother is a verb. It's something you do.

Not just who you are.

DOROTHY CANFIELD FISHER

Mother is the name for God
in the lips and hearts of little children.

WILLIAM MAKEPEACE THACKERAY

Biology is the least of what makes someone a mother.

Oprah Winfrey

Motherhood has a very humanizing effect.
Everything gets reduced to essentials.

MERYL STREEP

I'm not vicious really.

I consider myself kind-hearted.

I love my mum.

SID VICIOUS

All I am I owe to my mother.
I attribute all my success in life to the moral,
intellectual and physical education
I received from her.

George Washington

God could not be everywhere,

and therefore he made mothers.

Rudyard Kipling

I think this power of living in our children
is one of the sweetest things in the world . . .

LOUISA MAY ALCOTT

I am sure that if the mothers of various nations could meet,
there would be no more wars.

E.M. FORSTER

Pride is one of the seven deadly sins;

but it cannot be the pride of a mother in her children,

for that is a compound of two cardinal virtues – faith and hope.

CHARLES DICKENS

She was of the stuff of which
great men's mothers are made.
She was indispensable to high generation,
hated at tea parties, feared in shops,
and loved at crises.

Thomas Hardy

How beautifully everything is arranged by Nature;
as soon as a child enters the world,
it finds a mother ready to take care of it.

JULES MICHELET

Love as powerful as your mother's for you

leaves its own mark . . . to have been loved so deeply . . .

will give us some protection forever.

J.K. ROWLING

A babe, by intercourse of touch
I held mute dialogues with my Mother's heart.

WILLIAM WORDSWORTH

Right now, after giving birth, I really understand
the power of my body. I just feel my body means
something completely different.

BEYONCÉ

For we think back through our mothers if we are women.

Virginia Woolf

The Lord gives a good many things twice over,
but he don't give ye a mother but once.

Harriet Beecher Stowe

My mother used to say that there are no strangers, only friends you haven't met yet. She's now in a maximum security twilight home in Australia.

BARRY HUMPHRIES

If you knew how great is a mother's love,
you would have no fear.

J.M. BARRIE

Mama was my greatest teacher, a teacher
of compassion, love and fearlessness.
If love is sweet as a flower, then my mother
is that sweet flower of love.

Stevie Wonder

Life began with waking up
and loving my mother's face.

GEORGE ELIOT

Children are the anchors

that hold a mother to life.

Sophocles

I want my children to have all the things I couldn't afford.
Then I want to move in with them.

Phyllis Diller

For when a child is born
the mother also is born again.

GILBERT PARKER

For me, being a mother made me a better professional,
because coming home every night to my girls
reminded me what I was working for.

Michelle Obama

O Mother blest, whom God bestows

On sinners and on just,

What joy, what hope thou givest those

Who in thy mercy trust!

St Alphonsus, trans. by E. Vaughan

The most remarkable thing about my mother is that for thirty years she served the family nothing but leftovers. The original meal has never been found.

CALVIN TRILLIN

The mother's heart is the child's schoolroom.

HENRY WARD BEECHER

Let France have good Mothers,
and she will have good sons.

NAPOLEON I

But a mother's love endures through all;
in good repute, in bad repute,
in the face of the world's condemnation,
a mother still loves on . . .

Washington Irving

Her children arise up,
and call her blessed.

PROVERBS 31:28

I remember my mother's prayers and they have always followed me. They have clung to me all my life.

ABRAHAM LINCOLN

Men are what their mothers made them.

RALPH WALDO EMERSON

My mother is my root, my foundation.
She planted the seed that I base my life on,
and that is the belief that the ability to achieve
starts in your mind.

MICHAEL JORDAN

Sometimes the strength of motherhood
is greater than natural laws.

BARBARA KINGSOLVER

No matter how old a mother is,
she watches her middle-aged children
for signs of improvement.

FLORIDA SCOTT-MAXWELL

The memory of my mother and her teachings were,
after all, the only capital I had to start life with,
and on that capital I have made my way.

ANDREW JACKSON

Oh, what a power is motherhood, possessing

A potent spell

All women alike

Fight fiercely for a child.

EURIPIDES

Children and mothers never truly part –
Bound in the beating of each other's heart.

CHARLOTTE GRAY

Mother is the heartbeat in the home;
and without her,
there seems to be no heart throb.

LEROY BROWNLOW

A mother laughs our laughter,

Sheds our tears,

Returns our love,

Fears our fears.

She lives our joys,

Cares our cares,

And all our hopes and dreams she shares.

JULIA SUMMERS

Making the decision to have a child – it's momentous.
It is to decide forever to have your heart
go walking around outside your body.

ELIZABETH STONE

I think every working mom

probably feels the same thing . . .

'This is impossible – oh, this is impossible.'

And then you just keep going and keep going,

and you sort of do the impossible.

TINA FEY

The mother loves her child most divinely . . .
when she resolutely holds him to the highest standards
and is content with nothing less than his best.

HAMILTON WRIGHT MABIE

I looked on child-rearing not only as
a work of love and duty but as a profession
that was fully as interesting and challenging
as any honorable profession in the world . . .

ROSE KENNEDY

So for the mother's sake the child was dear,

And dearer was the mother for the child.

SAMUEL TAYLOR COLERIDGE

Love still has something of the sea

From whence his mother rose.

Charles Sedley

We have a beautiful
mother
Her green lap
immense
Her brown embrace
eternal
Her blue body
everything
we know.

ALICE WALKER

A wise son maketh a glad father:
but a foolish son is the heaviness
of his mother.

PROVERBS 10:1

Begin, baby boy,
to recognise your mother
with a smile.

VIRGIL

Who ran to help me when I fell,
And would some pretty story tell,
Or kiss the place to make it well?
My Mother.

ANN AND JANE TAYLOR

The story of a mother's life:

Trapped between a scream and a hug.

CATHY GUISEWITE

To describe my mother would be to write
about a hurricane in its perfect power.

MAYA ANGELOU

O wondrous power!

How little understood,

Entrusted to the mother's mind alone,

To fashion genius —

to form the soul for good.

Sarah Josepha Hale

For when you looked
into my mother's eyes
you knew.
as if He had told you,
why God had sent her into the world . . .
it was to open the minds of all
who looked to beautiful things.

J.M. BARRIE

There never was a child so lovely

but his mother was glad to get him asleep.

Ralph Waldo Emerson

The mother's yearning, that completest type
of the life in another life, which is the essence
of real human love, feels the presence
of the cherished child even
in the debased, degraded man.

GEORGE ELIOT

Mothers are a biological necessity;
fathers are a social invention.

Margaret Mead

My mother, she was my first friend
in the proper sense of the word.

NELSON MANDELA

There is nothing in the world of art
like the songs mother used to sing.

Billy Sunday

A mother is a mother still, the holiest thing alive.

SAMUEL TAYLOR COLERIDGE

Who's a boy gonna talk to
if not his mother?

There is none,

In all this cold and hollow world, no fount

Of deep, strong, deathless love, save that within

A mother's heart.

FELICIA HEMANS

I shall never forget my mother,
for it was she who planted and nurtured
the first seeds of good within me.

IMMANUEL KANT

If you desire to drain to the dregs
the fullest cup of scorn and hatred
that a fellow human being can pour
out for you, let a young mother hear you
call dear baby 'it'.

JEROME K. JEROME

My mother was the making of me.
She was so true and so sure of me,
I felt that I had someone to live for —
someone I must not disappoint.

THOMAS EDISON

When I stopped seeing my mother
with the eyes of a child,
I saw the woman who helped me
give birth to myself.

NANCY FRIDAY

I looked at my children and I said,
'These are my poems. These are my short stories.'

Olga Masters

If evolution really works,
how come mothers only have two hands?

MILTON BERLE

The most important thing
a father can do for his children
is to love their mother.

THEODORE HESBURGH

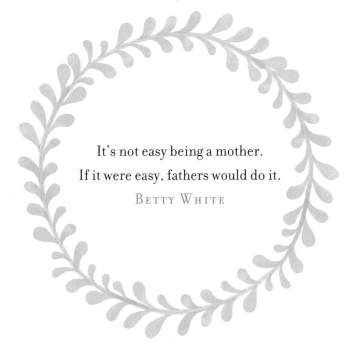

It's not easy being a mother.

If it were easy, fathers would do it.

Betty White

My mother . . . she is beautiful,

softened at the edges and tempered with a spine of steel.

I want to grow old and be like her.

Jodi Picoult

A mother's love for her child is like nothing else in the world.
It knows no law, no pity, it dares all things and
crushes down remorselessly all that stands in its path.

AGATHA CHRISTIE

I will look after you . . . I am here.

I brought my whole self to you. I am your mother.

Maya Angelou

A mother understands what a child does not say.

JEWISH PROVERB

Mother love is the fuel that enables
a normal human being to do the impossible.

MARION C. GARRETTY

A mother's happiness is like a beacon,
lighting up the future but reflected also
on the past in the guise of fond memories.

Honoré de Balzac

There's no way to be a perfect mother
and a million ways to be a good one.

JILL CHURCHILL

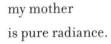

my mother
is pure radiance.

she is the sun
i can touch
and kiss

and hold
without
getting burnt.

SANOBER KHAN

But behind all your stories is
your mother's story, for hers
is where yours begins.

MITCH ALBOM

Women know
The way to rear up children (to be just)
They know a simple, merry, tender knack
Of tying sashes, fitting baby shoes,
And stringing pretty words that make no sense,
And kissing full sense into empty words.

Elizabeth Barrett Browning

Mother's love grows by giving.

CHARLES LAMB

A mother would have been
always present. A mother
would have been a constant
friend; her influence would
have been beyond all other.

JANE AUSTEN

I know how to do anything – I'm a mom.

Roseanne Barr

Mother: the most beautiful word
on the lips of mankind.

KAHLIL GIBRAN

You may have tangible wealth untold:
Caskets of jewels and coffers of gold.
Richer than I you can never be
I had a Mother who read to me.

STRICKLAND GILLILAN

Neurotics build castles in the air,
psychotics live in them.
My mother cleans them.

RITA RUDNER

Becoming a mother makes you
the mother of all children . . .
You long to comfort all who are
desolate.

CHARLOTTE GRAY

Everybody wants to save the Earth;
nobody wants to help Mom do the dishes.

P.J. O'ROURKE

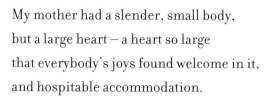

My mother had a slender, small body,
but a large heart — a heart so large
that everybody's joys found welcome in it,
and hospitable accommodation.

MARK TWAIN

[A] mother is one to whom you hurry
when you are troubled.

EMILY DICKINSON

My mother was the one constant in my life.

BARACK OBAMA

There's no such thing as a supermom.
We just do the best we can.

SARAH MICHELLE GELLAR